HAL LEONARD
STUDENT
PIANO
LIBRARY

More Christmas Piano Solos

For All Piano Methods

T0080105

Table of Contents

	Page No.	CD Track
Jolly Old St. Nicholas	2	1/2
Up on the Housetop	4	3/4
Away in a Manger	6	5/6
O Come, Little Children	8	7/8
I Saw Three Ships	10	9/10
Deck the Hall	12	11/12
The Huron Carol	14	13/14

Book: ISBN 978-1-4234-8360-1
Book/CD: ISBN 978-1-4234-9325-9

HAL•LEONARD®
CORPORATION

7777 W. BLUEMOUND RD. P.O. BOX 13819 MILWAUKEE, WI 53213

In Australia Contact:
Hal Leonard Australia Pty. Ltd.
4 Lentara Court
Cheltenham, Victoria, 3192 Australia
Email: ausadmin@halleonard.com.au

Visit Hal Leonard Online at
www.halleonard.com

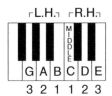

Jolly Old St. Nicholas

Traditional 19th Century American Carol
Arranged by Mona Rejino

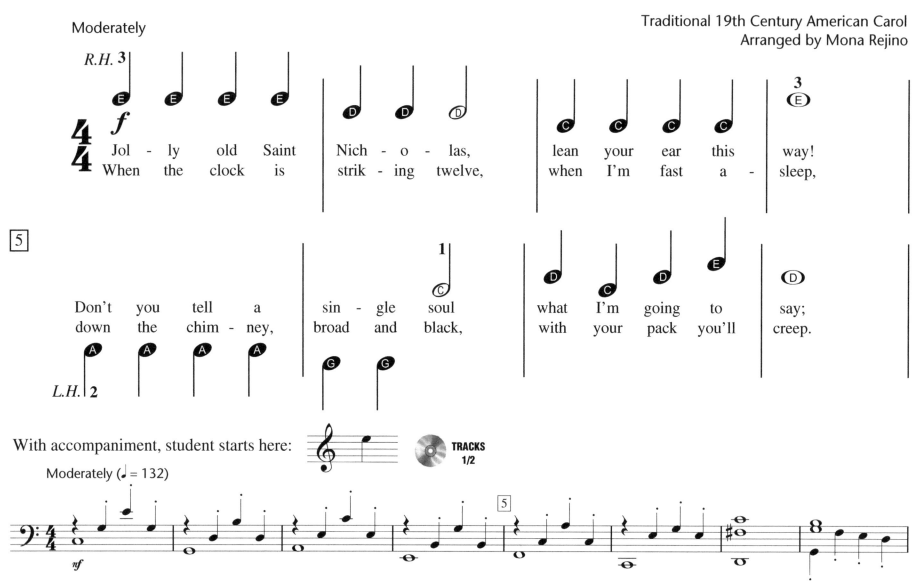

9 *R.H.* **3**

p

Christ - mas Eve is | com - ing soon, | now you dear old | man,
All the stock - ings | you will find | hang - ing in a | row;

13

whis - per what you'll | bring to me, | tell me if you | can.
mine will be the | short - est one, | you'll be sure to | know.

L.H. **2**

3

Up on the Housetop

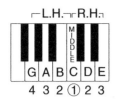

Words and Music by B.R. Hanby
Arranged by Fred Kern

With spirit

R.H.

Up on the house-top the rein - deer pause; out jumps good old San - ta Claus.

Down through the chim-ney with lots of toys, all for the little ones' Christ - mas joys!

With accompaniment, student starts here:

TRACKS 3/4

With spirit (♩ = 100)

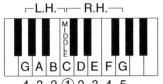

Away in a Manger

Words by John T. McFarland (v.3)
Music by James R. Murray
Arranged by Fred Kern

7

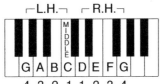

O Come, Little Children

Words by C. von Schmidt
Music by J.P.A. Schulz
Arranged by Mona Rejino

9

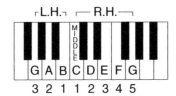

I Saw Three Ships

Traditional English Carol
Arranged by Phillip Keveren

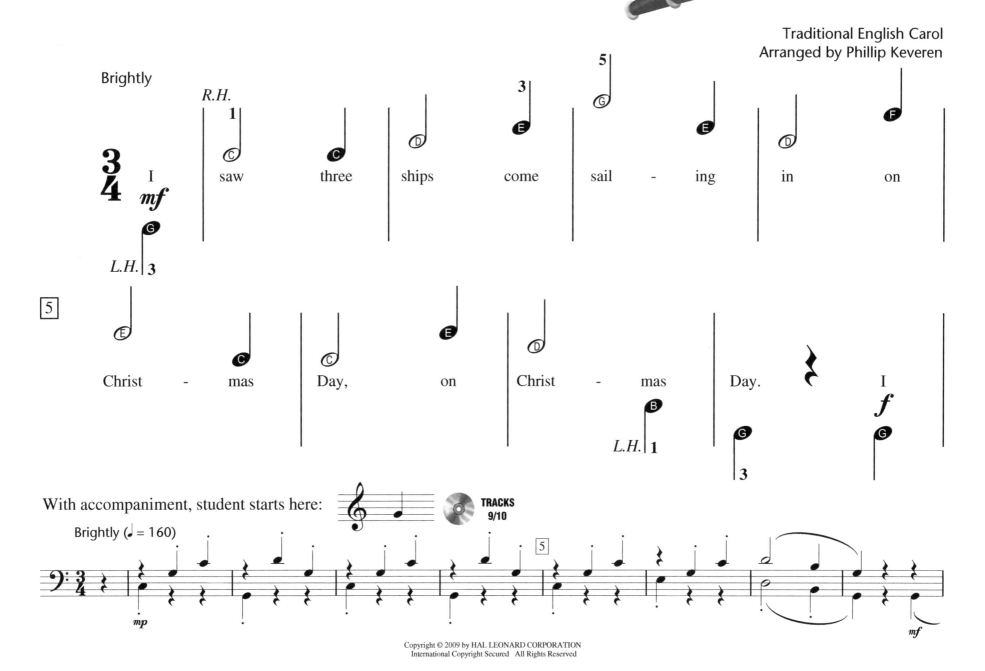

Brightly

R.H.

L.H.

I saw three ships come sail - ing in on

Christ - mas Day, on Christ - mas Day. I

With accompaniment, student starts here:

TRACKS 9/10

Brightly (♩ = 160)

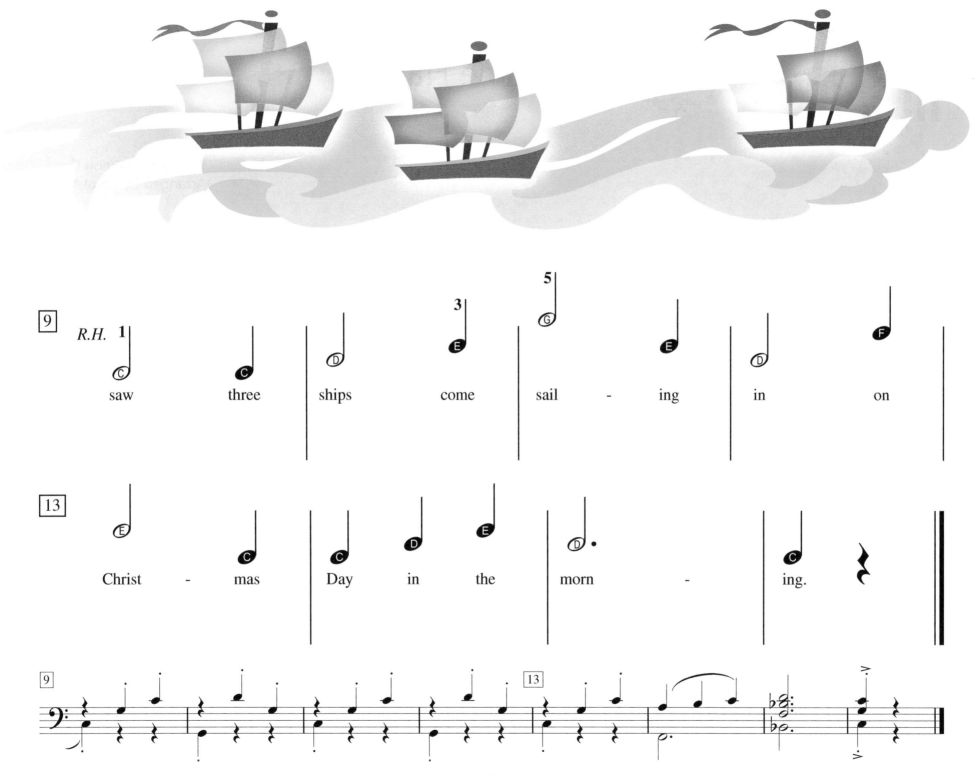

Deck the Hall

Traditional Welsh Carol
Arranged by Carol Klose

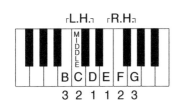

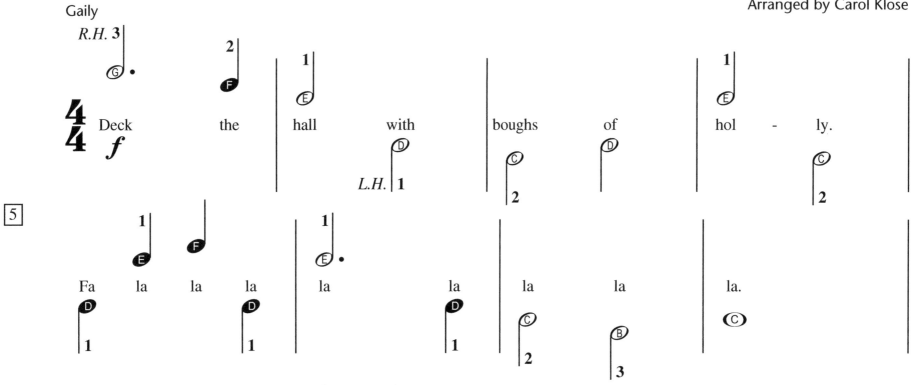

With accompaniment, student starts here:

TRACKS
11/12

Gaily (♩ = 120)

Optional: play both hands one octave higher to the end.

9 — 'Tis the sea - son to be jol - ly.

13 — Fa la la la la la la la la.

The Huron Carol

Traditional French-Canadian Text
Traditional Canadian-Indian Melody
Arranged by Jennifer Linn

'Twas in the moon of win - ter - time when all the birds had fled, that

With accompaniment, student starts here:

TRACKS 13/14

Steady (♩ = 112)

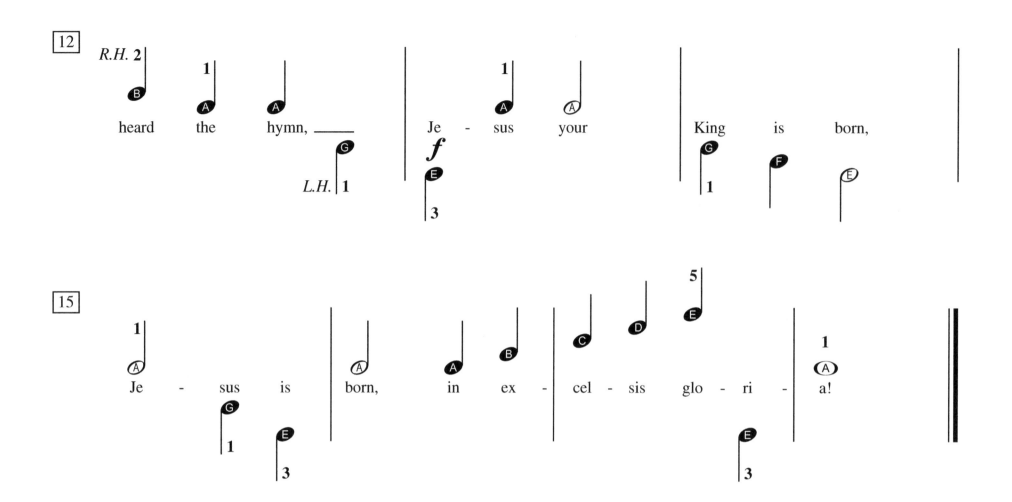